"We Tried That Once"

And Other Popular Excuses
That Sabotage Business Success!

"Leadership Larry" Mietus

RPSS Publishing - Buffalo, New York

RPSS Publishing - Buffalo, New York

DEDICATION

To my wife Kathy (my best friend, my soul mate, and the love of my life), I will never have the words to express all that you mean to me. Your faith and trust in me have always allowed me to pursue my entrepreneurial endeavors. Thanks for bringing sunshine into every life you touch.

To our children, Desiree', Ryan and John. You have taught me more about life than I will ever be able to teach you. You each have wonderful qualities that I try to emulate. I have learned patience and persistence from each of you along with being a friend to the "under dog".

I love you and I will always be proud of you.

CONTENTS

Chapter 1

"We Tried That Once"

We live in a results driven world. Often, we're bogged down "fighting fires" in our business and personal lives. It's that firefighting mode and treading water so we don't drown that can stifle creativity and innovation. As an independent business consultant my clients count on me to drive creativity and innovation within their companies. My view is unjaded because I don't live in the forest with the trees where my clients live. I also have the advantage of not being emotionally or politically involved as the people who work in the organization (as they should be). Although I pride myself on being a professional, I don't get hung up on being too "politically correct". The reality is that I often get to ask the questions, make the observations and eventually offer the recommendations that employees would like to, but they fear retribution for speaking out (hours cut, less than desirable assignments, getting fired, etc.).

Casual conversations and even some properly conducted brainstorming sessions typically elicit ideas. Some of the ideas I offer up to clients are met with a resounding chorus of "We tried that once." My response usually is "Really, just once?" In defense of themselves the clients' responses to that question include statements such as "It was a dumb idea", "No one really was in favor of trying that", "Our customers wouldn't go for that" or "We knew it wouldn't work from the beginning."

Now don't get me wrong, sometimes there is validity behind some of those statements. However often statements such as those suggest a lack of discipline, an improper brainstorming process, inappropriate allocation of resources or simply impatience with the processes of innovation.

Many of the greatest discoveries and accomplishments known to "humankind" were the result of multiple prototypes, tests, focus groups and experiments. The thought of "We tried that once" may have crossed the minds of determined women and men throughout history but it did not deter them from achieving their goals.

Success was not without toil for James Dyson (over 5,000 vacuum cleaner prototypes), Thomas Edison (some teachers told him he was "too stupid to learn anything" yet he has over 1,000 patents to his name), Walt Disney (who was once told he lacked imagination), Elvis (who was advised to go back to driving a truck after his first performance at the Grand Ole Opry), Michael Jordan (cut from his high school basketball team) and Henry Ford (you might be driving one) who was quoted as saying "Failure is simply the opportunity to begin again, this time more intelligently". Buffalo, New York's musical icons the Goo Goo Dolls cranked out tunes for roughly a decade before the song "Name" made the band's name a household name.

It's easy (and human) to "throw in the towel" or "wave the white flag". However, the people and organizations that work through challenges and adversity are the ones who ultimately can proclaim "We did it!" I totally understand that sometimes we run out of money, patience, time or all three. We encounter obstacles we didn't anticipate (sometimes as the result of improper research) or we just don't have the intellectual resources under our roof that an idea or project requires. And yes, plain old bad luck does exist.

All that said, proper planning still prevents poor performance. Do your homework. It costs nothing but time to ask people "What do you think of the following idea….?" Be careful of course who you ask questions of or who you share information with. As trusting as most humans like to be there are still unscrupulous people out there who will steal your ideas in a heartbeat and claim them as their own. The use of nondisclosure agreements (NDAs) is often a recommendation I make to my clients. Your attorney can draft one or you can modify one that you find online.

Take Action Tips:

- Create and maintain an atmosphere where everyone believes there are no dumb ideas.
- Do your homework (research and due diligence). See Chapter 8.
- Brainstorm what could go wrong with your idea.
- Brainstorm what could go right with your idea.
- Be careful not to overthink, over analyze, and stall out your momentum (that's typically when your competition passes you by).
- Set timelines for progress with achievement milestones (what will be accomplished by when).
- Plan for capital if needed (your own or borrowed money from traditional lenders, alternative funding lenders, or investors).
- Expect that nothing will roll out the way you planned it.
- Learn from your mistakes and the feedback you receive from your team, friends, family, and investors and move on.
- Don't do the easy thing. Don't fall into the lazy mental trap and comfort zone of saying "We tried that once."
- Be persistent!

Chapter 2

"No One Will Notice"

Sometimes we get lazy. Myself included. Good enough will do so we go with that. Sometimes good enough is cheaper, faster, and easier. Every now and then good enough is acceptable as we measure an activity's return versus the investment expense of people, time, and money (ROI).

The fact of the matter is lots of people notice plenty of things. Our customers, clients, patients, friends, family members, and competitors take notice. Does it seem like there's less cereal in that box and more air for the higher price you're paying? Is it taking longer for your people to answer the phones at work and are they rushing customers off the phone? Is your facility not as clean as it used to be? Are there misspelled words or broken links on your organization's web site? Yes, people notice.

The little things do count. Aim for small strides and continuous improvement. Sometimes there's a fine line between justified complacency and the laziness trap. In the lifecycle of business (read more in Chapter 7) most companies start out by overpaying for just about everything so they can get in the game (talent, people, raw materials, space, equipment etc.). In time these companies stabilize because they now have established customers, better purchasing leverage and hopefully the knowledge they've gained from experience which allows them to quote and bid more accurately along with the ability to control costs more effectively.

Mature businesses run the risk of getting "fat, dumb and happy!" That's when and where the mentality of "No one will notice" usually creeps in. We cut corners for the sake of "efficiency", we alter ingredients for the sake of cost, and we deliver substandard customer service because our customers "aren't complaining". Run in the comfort zone too long without a plan for strategic growth and improvement and suddenly you wake up to the company in a nosedive with your lender ready to call your loan and your competitors sprinting past you to the bank to make the deposits you used to make.

You know the drill. If your customers, clients, or patients notice the wrong things they'll tell lots of people (perhaps via social media). If they are talking about your company because they noticed the right things they won't tell as many people as if they were unhappy. Those whispers can cascade into a chorus of praise for your company accompanied by the sweet sound of the cash register ringing! However human nature dictates that people go into full broadcast mode when they are not happy with your product, service, or lack of customer service. Sometimes it becomes a personal vendetta for an unhappy customer to grind their axe with your company and generate as much negative publicity for you as they possibly can.

It can take a lot of time to deal with an upset customer, calm them on social media platforms and manage your online reputation. We live in a digital and virtual world. You should absolutely be spending time and money promoting your company on social media. Why not promote all the good things you're doing? Your company's new products. Your company's new services. Your company's commitment to the community.

People notice. Give them the right reasons to take notice.

Take Action Tips:

- Work like everyone is watching and know that people see, hear about, and talk about your business more than you think they do.
- Comments and concerns from the staff and customers should be reviewed by top level management every day and acted upon accordingly.
- Improve your product. Make consistent small improvements (Think Lean, Six Sigma, Kaizen). One degree of "better" may be all you need to put some distance between you and your competitors.
- Bolster your services.
- Innovate. Create. Ask "why not"?
- Hire the best people available in the marketplace at the time you have a hiring need. Yes, you may have missed someone exceptionally talented yesterday and there will certainly be a "rock star" becoming available tomorrow but there's someone out there who can play "lead guitar" in your workplace band today. Know your "policy" when it comes to recruiting or hiring from a competitor and abide by it.
- Keep your eyes open for talented people as you encounter them from any industry or walk of life. Having a "mental pipeline" of where talented people currently work can make recruiting less frustrating when the time comes to flip the switch on the "We're Hiring" sign.
- Create a mindset of permanent recruiting. Not as a threat to the team in place but as an ongoing commitment to employ the best talent.

Chapter 3

"It's Not My Job (Not My Problem)"

Jobs (positions) need accurate and contemporary job descriptions. Companies also need employee handbooks and organizational charts. All these tools add clarity to who does what, what exactly "what" is, and how the chains of communication and authority flow within an organization. However, the danger of job descriptions is that sometimes people hide behind theirs. Instead of "pitching in" whenever and wherever they can, they limit their thoughts, actions, and accountabilities to their individual job duties.

Effective leaders (those who build the culture, empower people, trust people, drive change and focus on results) make it clear that certain "jobs" belong to EVERYONE in the company. That thought can often be guided by clear mission and vision statements. That said, I'm not overly concerned with my client companies that don't have great (or any) mission and vision statements. My preference would be that they have statements which address Employee Obligation, Ethics, and Customer Service. How about rolling those into one statement of Core Values?

In some way, shape or form many people follow sports teams at some level. I love to listen to Monday conversations in workplaces after weekends filled with sporting events. If someone's favorite team won over the weekend, they usually say "We won!" (as if they participated in getting the job done). If their favorite team lost people say, "They lost!" (no fault of mine). Ever experience those sentiments at work across people, departments, or divisions when the wins and losses are being tallied up?

At work there should be responsibilities and commitments that belong to all of us. There should also be some element of cross training in organizations so people can discover what role they could potentially fill next (or at least you have backup if someone takes ill or jumps ship). Cross training is a great way to build bench strength and potentially alleviate job burnout. A new set of eyes may also bring about some fresh ideas in an area where thought processes and activity may have become stagnant.

Employee engagement prominently figures into this particular excuse. People who are not engaged at work will most likely throw the "It's not my job" card on the table more often than their counterparts who are engaged.

Probe for engagement traits during the interview process. Were job candidates simply showing up for work at their previous place of employment? What tasks have they taken on at work that were not part of their job descriptions? How active are they in the community? Ask what motivates them or how do they motivate themselves?

Remember there is a difference between a job and a career. Many people are perfectly content to work a job that enables them to provide for themselves and/or their families. They may want limited authority and limited responsibility and may not have any interest at all in upward mobility. That's fine. The workforce needs those workers. It's better to identify the aspirations and intentions of employees sooner than later and revisit engagement levels regularly.

Take Action Tips:

• Make sure that your company has an organizational chart and that it is reviewed and updated regularly (2-4 times per year should suffice depending on the rate of change within your company).

• "Pencil in" on the organizational chart the positions that do not currently exist but may need to be developed/added as your company pivots, expands or contracts.

• Be certain that job descriptions are accurate and contemporary.

• Identify the "hungry learners" in your company and keep "feeding them." Tuition assistance, online courses, and upskilling are all worth their weight in gold and may also fuel employee attraction and retention efforts. Involve them in projects.

• Cross train religiously.

Chapter 4

"That Would Never Work Here"

As businesspeople we often read, see, and witness the great things that companies can accomplish because they are giants (Amazon, Google, UPS, Walmart etc.). It's tempting (and easy) to observe some of those policies, procedures, marketing strategies, and community commitments and say "if we were that big" or "had that much money" or "had people who knew how to do that" …"we'd do the same thing!"

That's where scaling comes in. Pick one of those great things that the "players" do and study it. Chunk it down so its fits your company. Make it your own. Put your unique spin on it. High school sports teams now run plays that used to be run by collegiate teams. Collegiate teams run plays that used to be reserved for the pros. What can you add to your corporate playbook? Ask your customers. Rest assured they'll have ideas on what features or services they'd like to see your company start offering.

A word of caution. Don't bite off more than you can chew. Be realistic when planning. Depending on the size and scope of the change you'd like to implement make sure that your plans are reasonable. When it comes to planning for change you'll want to consider your resources such as your organization's intellectual horsepower, capital available for the project, production capabilities, fulfillment and storage, and available time. Be aware of any government or industry regulations (including proposed or pending ones) and current competition.

We're talking about making a change. A change that you believe will have a positive impact on your company. Perhaps a change that will increase revenue, decrease costs, improve customer satisfaction, or increase market share. No matter what you're striving for as you move down the path of change you need to be aware of the emotions that you and your team will experience. If you expect the following stages of change and the emotions that accompany them you will increase the probability of your planned change(s) becoming successful reality.

Forming:
You put the "ball in play". A change is discussed or announced. The status quo is rocked.

Storming:
People complain as humans will. Humans resist change as is well documented and experienced every day. Tell yourself to expect this emotion. The good news is that just like the weather, storming doesn't last forever.

Norming:
Ah, things are calming down. This new idea, action, policy, or behavior is starting to take hold. People aren't as resistant as they once were. The "new normal" is taking hold.

Performing:
At this stage it's quite clear that the change isn't the "flavor of the month" …it is NOT going away and we're getting good at executing it. The team is hitting stride!

Adjourning:

This stage is sometimes overlooked by organizations or simply not anticipated. Sometimes we need to dismantle the team that was assembled to create, foster, and drive the change because their work is done. Mission accomplished! Be aware of the fact that that team had a life of its own. The people on it bonded and took satisfaction in the work they produced. Sometimes it hurts when the team members realize they won't be collaborating the way they used to.

The change itself may actually be short lived (a temporary fix to a temporary challenge) so when the once "new" idea, action, policy, or behavior is repealed the same sense of deflation may set in among your associates. Your customers may also experience the same sense of deflation (especially if they liked the change). Be careful with what you tinker with. Be strategic.

If trust does not exist between employees and senior leadership change efforts will be difficult to say the least. Trust reduces fear, encourages a risk-taking mentality, and minimizes the suspicion of ulterior motives.

Take Action Tips:

• Companies that don't plan on changing are planning on stagnating or perhaps even failing. Be open to ideas and possibilities. It's a slippery downward slope when change on the outside is greater than change on the inside.

• Change doesn't have to be monumental. Sometimes small tweaks on an existing product or service are all you need. Large scale change can be glamorous, but it isn't always practical.

• Be open to not only the best practices of companies within your industry but the best practices of the most successful companies in general.

• Embrace trial periods and probationary exercises (piloting). If something new doesn't work, you can usually go back to what you did in the past.

• Set limits on the time, effort, energy, and monies you'll invest in an effort to try something new. Know when to pull the plug. Hope springs eternal but it's unbridled hope that can fuel financial distress.

• Trying something new requires consensus. Consensus does not mean that everyone is in agreement with the new idea. It does mean that everyone agrees not to sabotage the effort moving forward. Your plan may fail. If it does the hardcore naysayers will most certainly let you know that they "knew it would fail" all along.

Chapter 5

"I Don't Have Time to Meet with Employees"

I once read an article that detailed the responses of CEOs who were surveyed about how they spend their time during the course of a 40-hour work week (if such a thing exists at the "C" level). Several CEOs reported that they spent approximately 16 hours (2 days) per week dealing with people or people issues. What surprised me was the fact that many of them were complaining about that reality.

I always teach and preach that "people are the greatest resource that any organization has, period!" Your company might have a brand-new building, state of the art technology, and great advertising and marketing. But if a CEO, leader, or manager showed up at work tomorrow and they were the only person there how would the enterprise function? How does the company operate? Exactly!

People are a priority. The #1 priority. That's where plenty of time needs to be INVESTED. For years I've said that the higher you climb up the proverbial corporate ladder the less you need to know about processes, prices and policies and the more you need to know about building and maintaining meaningful relationships with people…the ones who work with you (not for you), the ones who purchase from you, the ones who can refer or recommend, you and the ones who can connect you. (Remember to do the same for them!) Behind every sophisticated piece of technology or technological breakthrough stands people. Humans with emotions still trump robots and artificial intelligence.

As a consultant I've witnessed plenty of organizations where there is a disconnect between managers, leaders, owners, and the associates (or some combination of this dysfunction). This simply is NOT acceptable. At the end of the day most people don't require much to feel a sense of satisfaction at work that is fueled by a healthy level of engagement. Our careers at work often follow this pattern. We get out of school (high school or college) and we land a job. Our primary goals are to earn enough money to be able to buy clothes that are nice enough to wear to work, drive a dependable vehicle (one that starts every day) and hopefully have some money left over for entertainment. Moving into our own place…dream come true. Time goes by, we "pay our dues" and "climb the ladder" with the hope that every new rung of responsibility brings an increase in earnings. We can finally afford to knock things off our bucket lists.

But one day we awaken yearning for some things that money can't buy. At work we want to be respected. We want our voices to be heard. We want our opinions to count and perhaps we desire to coach or mentor someone else in our organization or profession. We want attention and appreciation especially from managers, leaders, and owners.

The Millennial generation now comprises the largest sector of the American workforce. Millennials report that they want to have regular access to competent leaders at work early in their careers. (Day number 2 would be good). Leaders, managers, and owners need to make that happen. I'm frequently asked by business owners if they "have to" hire Millennials because the owners don't understand them, can't manage them, and generally think Millennials are entitled and lazy. My response is always "Of course you don't have to hire them. If you're planning on going out of business in the not too distant future don't hire any of them."

Take Action Tips:

- As a CEO or owner you need to get involved in the hiring process at the onset. It makes a powerful impression when a job candidate meets an owner during the first or second visit. That gesture sets a tone that says you are accessible (make sure you are moving forward) and speaks directly to your company's culture.

- Some of you may remember Managing by Walking Around (Tom Peters). Take a daily lap around the office or plant. Chat briefly with people. Smile. Acknowledge their efforts. Thank them for coming to work today. At times a simple nod of the head and wave of the hand will let people know you care and you're aware. If your organization is multilocation reach out to people via intranet, ZOOM, or social media. (Some old dogs will need to learn new tricks).

- Spend quality time with your people. Learn what motivates them. Show interest in their habits and their hobbies. Know what "makes them tick." "Break bread" with them. Understand their fears and concerns. Listen to their complaints and suggestions.

- Recruit, hire, retain and promote to your culture. Yes, that absolutely takes more time, but the positive results are well worth the investment of time.

- Be careful of what you say and do with regard to your employees for reasons of cultural cultivation, morale, and business, civil, and criminal laws.

- Lead by positive and proactive example, not by offering excuses.
- Praise in public. Chastise in private.
- Encourage people to challenge you respectfully.
- Don't surround yourself with "yes" people.
- Take no one for granted. Everyone has unique skills, experiences, and perspectives.
- Take chances on potential front runners. Accelerate the growth curve for high potential individuals if they are interested (they may not be). You may not always be right regarding their abilities but that beats frustrating someone to the point where they leave your organization due to perceived or actual stagnation.

Chapter 6

"I Don't Like Conflict"

Raise your hand if you woke up this morning with the sole goal of creating conflict today. Experience tells me that there is only a 10% - 15% chance that your hand is up. Conflict makes most people uncomfortable. We typically don't seek conflict. We don't embrace it. Many people go to great lengths to avoid it. Sometimes we run and hide from it.

Conflict avoidance is rooted in the fact that when most people hear the term "conflict" they associate it with yelling, screaming, arguing, stress, a sharp disagreement, a lack of harmony, and potentially damaged relationships. Those associations are indeed accurate when we're talking about dysfunctional conflict. When we keep our thoughts and feelings inside of our heads in our efforts to avoid conflict, we run the risks of pulling away, shutting down, becoming less productive, less creative, and potentially damaging our physical and mental health.

The other side of the conflict coin is functional conflict. The kind of conflict that when managed appropriately can foster learning opportunities, make relationships stronger, create better solutions to challenges, and maybe even lower your blood pressure a few points.

Our perceptions of conflict and how we manage it were ingrained in most of us starting at an early age. We watched how our families managed conflict, often around the dinner table. We heard about how conflict was avoided or managed from our parents who told us stories about their places of work. We gained a sense of our own conflict boundaries as individuals. History, politics, emotions, stereotypes, education, environment, and our physical and mental state all fuel our approach to conflict.

Society adjusts its compass with regard to conflict every so often. I grew up during the Vietnam era. Not a day went by for years that the word "war" wasn't in a newspaper headline. Today we refer to wars between people and countries as conflicts. Perhaps we've deescalated our sensitivity level too much?

How we handle conflict is sometimes guided by rules, laws, policies, and procedures. Your own personal stake in the outcome of a perceived (there may actually be no conflict even though you anticipated one) or real conflict will dictate how much time, effort, and energy you put into navigating conflict. The amount of time you have to deal with conflict, your interpersonal communication skills, and your negotiation skills all impact your willingness to engage in conflict and manage it at a functional level.

Take some time to reflect upon your personal conflict management style. Do you run from conflict? Do you acquiesce every time to everyone else? Are you a collaborator who works with others to manage conflict from a positive perspective in an effort to reach the most fruitful outcomes? Are you a skilled negotiator who seeks wins for everyone at the table and not just yourself? Are you a dictator forcing your will upon others while wielding a "take it or leave it" attitude?

Take Action Tips:

• Take the time to assess where you currently stand when it comes to conflict. Decide where you want to fall on the spectrum between functional and dysfunctional conflict moving forward and work to get to that place. Remember that as you ascend the ranks of leadership there is an expectation that you will seek to create functional conflict and not work to avoid conflict at all costs.

• Grow your emotional intelligence. Emotions obviously are a significant part of the conflict equation. The better you can understand yourself, control yourself, pick up on the emotions of others, and genuinely relate to people better, the greater your chances of mastering functional conflict.

• Treat everyone with courtesy and respect. I have a friend and colleague who is a professionally trained butler and successful business advisor. He always says, "You should treat all others with courtesy and respect." You may not agree with some people. You may not like them per se, and they may not necessarily like you. But if you treat others with courtesy and respect you can't be wrong for doing that.

• Go directly to the source (or attempt to communicate with them) who is creating the conflict. Avoid the water cooler, back-stabbing conversations that resonate throughout the halls of the places we call work. The only time I advise not going directly to the source is if that individual directly supervises you and you suspect or know that they are involved in illegal, unethical, or immoral behavior. In those situations, seek assistance from other individuals with some level of authority within your organization.

• Deal with the facts. The rumor mill will always be open and ripe for fuel. Facts help to paint a much clearer picture. Make sure your facts are accurate.

• Determine the root cause(s) of conflict and work to make changes that may potentially reduce potential conflict in the future. Often, we waste time engaged in dysfunctional conflict fueled by situations that were never rectified the first time they became situations.

• Focus on positive outcomes. A "win" for all parties involved in the conflict will not be possible 100% of the time but that's not a good reason to abandon that goal.

• Bury the past and move on. The study of gender intelligence teaches us that men are actually more ready, willing, and able to bury the past and move on versus their female counterparts. That said the emotional intelligence, long term memories, and recognition of patterns serve females in business much better than their male counterparts.

• The parties involved in the conflict should work together to resolve it. Conflict resolution is not a homework assignment to be handed out and collected a few days later. It's a dialogue. It's a process that gets refined over time.

• Remember that change can be a major driver of conflict. Be prepared for the emotional stages of change previously outlined in Chapter 4.

Chapter 7

"If It's Not Broken, Why Fix It?"

Complacency. It can sneak up on an organization. It can be prevalent in a company that is doing well…solid market share, steady sales, and profitability. We humans are creatures of habit. In our defense the greatest ability the human brain has is to recognize patterns. So, the more we can function "robotically" the less thinking we do. Sounds convenient. Sounds dangerous!

We often don't think about changing things up, making things better (even subtle changes) or attempting innovation unless we are forced to (we are losing customers, losing sales, watching profits drop, losing market share, etc.)

I'm referring to diversification. Not the type of diversification that many of us grew up with at work. That being diversity of people. Do we employ people who don't look like us? Do we employ people that don't dress like us? Do we have colleagues from different ethnic, religious, socio-economic, and sexual identification backgrounds than our own? No, not those critical differences. I'm suggesting operational diversification.

The life cycle of businesses typically looks something like this.
• Rush to "get into the game" or enter the industry. At this stage we typically overpay for just about everything (talent, working space, equipment, services, etc.). We do this because the longer we wait the more time goes by that we're not generating revenue. (Caution: Don't confuse generating revenue with generating profit!)

• Growing the business. We are bringing in new business and retaining more of our customers and clients then we are losing. We have a better handle on expenses. Perhaps we've negotiated better terms/deals with our vendors or replaced some of our initial vendors with ones that serve us better and have better terms.

• Mature business. The company isn't necessarily on "auto-pilot" but there are days when it feels like it is. Things are steady, revenue is predictable, and profitability is within the target range for our industry, our own projections or both. Customer satisfaction levels (for those who take the time to measure) are solid. Employee retention is normal or better for your industry. Things are comfortable. DANGEROUSLY COMFORTABLE!

The mature stage of business is exactly the place where business owners, leaders and employees fall asleep! It's a warm and fuzzy sleep. Things have been so good for so long that it's easy to just roll over and hit the "corporate snooze button" again.

The mature stage of business is the moment of truth. You should be strategically planning for innovation, creativity, and change within your operations. Focus on fueling constant growth. If you don't plan for improvement you run the risk of falling asleep at the wheel.

There have been numerous times in my career (both as an employee and a business consultant) where I've witnessed companies shocked into the reality of sliding sales, plummeting profits, and exiting employees and customers. Sometimes the nosedive is too deep, and the business can't level out. Lights out. Doors locked. Jobs lost.

Sometimes in these situations the "powers that be" have said "We didn't see that coming!" Of course not. How could you have? You were sleeping!

Take Action Tips:

- Know your competitors as well as you know your own company. Sam Walton said he'd got his best ideas from visiting his competitors' stores.
- Don't wait for your competitors or the market to force your hand to make changes to your business. Force yourself. If your business is struggling, make every attempt to strengthen it. If your business is good make it great. If your business is great make it exceptional.
- Stay on top of the data that tells the story of your industry. Know how to acquire it, interpret it, and plan from it. Are you and your company the "go to" subject matter experts in your industry? Do you know what it takes to be thought of that way?
- Swim upstream on occasion. Be creative. Seek innovative thoughts from ALL the people within your organization. Game changing ideas can come from people without expense accounts, designated parking spaces, and corner offices.
- "Break things" on purpose. Call your own customer service hotline. Visit your own locations or work sites. Have your product shipped to your home. Eat with your team in the cafeteria. Find things that are "broken" and fix them.

Chapter 8

"Everyone is Doing It!" (Or Buying It!)

Why not follow the crowd? After all some of those companies or individuals who are part of the crowd may have done the homework, done the research, built the prototypes, and surveyed the public prior to launching a product or service similar to the product or service you want to roll out. Maybe some of them did the "heavy lifting". Maybe.

It takes patience (especially if you're an entrepreneur) to conduct due diligence. Entrepreneurs are excited by what "could be". They envision high demand along with stellar sales for the products and services they've dreamed up. Don't we all? Who wouldn't want what we offer? "They" don't know what they're missing if they pass on what we bring to the market.

How many times have the words "Everyone is doing it" rolled off the lips of a teenager you know (or perhaps your lips at one point in your life)? Think back to those days when you were a teen under the control of your parents but trying to establish your identity, carve your own path, and fit in with the crowd. Smoking cigarettes…" Everyone is doing it!" Underage drinking…" Everyone is doing it!" Blowing past your curfew…" Everyone is doing it!" Vaping…you get the point. Over the years there were times when my wife and I had questions regarding certain activities of our children. Sometimes those questions were met with the chorus of "Everyone is doing it!" We usually responded with two questions. Who is everyone? Who are everyone's parents?

Fact of the matter is many people do many things both right and wrong. In the United States we encourage and protect freedom of choice. The question is do we learn lessons from the choices we make both personally and professionally?

Ethics hopefully guide our choices as people. Sometimes in business, people and organizations lower their ethical standards in order to make more profit or gain a first to market advantage. It's been proven that the temptation to lower corporate ethical standards is the greatest when a privately held company goes public and now must report actual performance numbers against projected performance numbers. Odd, unethical and at times illegal behaviors can sometimes surface during attempts to bolster the spirits of investors and shareholders. Remember the Enron, Adelphia, and Volkswagen scandals?

The greatest consequence to lowering your ethical standards may be what your internal team ends up thinking as opposed to the outside world. Decisions to act with less than ethical behavior can reduce employee loyalty and pride and end up having employees questioning if they are working for the right company. Take the high road. Take the legal road.

Let's shift gears to innovation and creativity. I believe that innovation means we came up with a new concept or a new twist on an old concept. Creativity in my mind is how we take that innovation and make it attractive to other people.

Is everyone doing "it" or buying "it" because your product, service or company has created a media tsunami? Today marketing gurus rack their brains trying to conjure up the next "thing" that will go viral. Oddly enough companies sometimes spend massive sums of money trying to generate media buzz while some of the most effective and memorable messages are born out of innocence (or accident) with no budget…just the right Tweet at the right time! Are your innovations and creations causing people to think "I need this now." "How did I survive without this?" "Why didn't I know about this sooner?"

Take Action Tips:

• Take the time to do the research. Your "great new idea" may already be living a healthy life of its own halfway around the world. Your projected numbers regarding potential market share may be extremely exaggerated. Ask the pioneers who are working to "mainstream" the growth, harvesting and sales of legalized marijuana.

• Make up your mind. Do you want to be an innovator, an early adaptor, a fence straddler or a laggard within your industry?

• Stick to what you do best. Make modifications to take those concepts, products, or services to the next level.

• Either run narrow and deep or wide and shallow. Your organization doesn't have the time, talent, money, or resources to do both.

• Survey the "person on the street". Ask simple questions such as "Would you purchase a product that _____?" How much would you be willing to pay for_____?"

• If the scope of the project, price of development, size of the loan or level of risk (or some combination thereof) associated with your new idea is significant; invest the money to conduct professionally led consumer focus groups to gain invaluable insights early on.

• Price cutting often falls into the "Everyone is doing it" category. There is no winner in the race to the bottom. Price is not a sustainable commodity, value is.

• Pay attention to what resonates with people. What stirs their emotions? What causes them to take action? The words you and yours continue to be two of the most powerful words in advertising. Let's not forget other time-tested favorites such as save, healthy, proven, and guaranteed. Remember to under promise and over deliver. Many people do the opposite!

"My Accountant Handles That"

Accounting. Not a word that brings smiles to many faces. Some of you may have taken an accounting course or two in college. If it was required for your major course of study, you most likely took those classes earlier along the path of your matriculating curriculum. If accounting wasn't required for your major but you took it anyway (God bless you) you waited as long as you could before buckling down to learn about debits, credits and financial ratios.

I believe that there are truly people who love to "crunch the numbers" and live to create pivot tables in Excel. I respect those individuals. Some of those folks are my friends and I admire their passion for their profession. At times I call them to work with some of my business clients when "deep dive" accounting analysis or assistance are needed.

When I use the term "accounting" I'm actually referring to a broader scope of knowledge that may actually be better described as financial acumen. Things like revenue, expenses, journal entries, job costing, inventory, accounts receivable, accounts payable, income statement, cash flow, balance sheet, assets, liabilities, cost of goods sold, equity, net income, trial balance, profit and loss statement, quick ratio, working capital ratio, liquidity ratio, and the future value of money. How many of those terms can you loosely define in your own words?

There was a point in my life when I couldn't define or describe any of them. But an Executive Finance course in my Organizational Leadership Master's degree program tripped my switch. The instructor launched the course by telling us that if we were to ascend to leadership roles inside of organizations, we had better ramp up our financial acumen. We did not have to be the people who populated the cells of an Excel spreadsheet but we had better be able to read financial documents, detect irregularities, recognize trends, and ask good questions of the people preparing those statements for the organization. If we were someday working for a publicly traded company and had the authority to sign off on financial documents and those documents were incorrect or falsified it was our fannies that could ultimately be sent to jail. Enter the Sarbanes-Oxley Act of 2002. I still don't "love the numbers" but I'm much more comfortable around them and certainly more proficient with them.

Truth be told it's the lack of financial acumen that gets companies into trouble. We assume that people who are intelligent and devoted enough to get through law school, medical school, or most MBA programs understand financials. The fact is many of them don't. As a mentor and reactor at the State University of New York at Buffalo's Center for Entrepreneurial Leadership I've found the common denominator among the waves of business entrepreneurs who have come through the program is the fact that they have little or no financial acumen and sometimes not much interest in developing it.

Hence, we put our faith and trust in people who "went to school for that." It's that faith and trust that can sometimes backfire. I've seen it numerous times throughout my career. Hard working, entrepreneurial women and men whose businesses are not as financially successful as they could or should be because they lack financial acumen. As long as there is enough money to cover payroll and vendors aren't knocking on the front door looking for payments, they assume everything is fine financially. I've sat in partner meetings at businesses where executives signed off on monthly financial reports without reading them, without asking questions, and without doing the math to see if the numbers tied out. It's as though the financial piece is a burden and not part of the strategic roadmap. One of my consulting peers who is a CPA always says "The numbers tell a story. Can you read the story?" "What actions will you take based upon the story?"

Take Action Tips:

• Increase your financial acumen. There are plenty of resources to enable you to do so. Books, classes, online courses, tutors, and consultants are all available at varying levels and costs to help you acquire more knowledge (see the next chapter). Contact me directly for my book recommendations on this subject area.

• Know what type of accounting/financial talent you need on your team. There's a difference between a Staff Accountant, Accounting Manager, Director of Accounting, VP of Accounting, Comptroller, and a Chief Financial Officer. One size does not fit all. The roles and responsibilities differ along with the levels of compensation.

• Meet (or least speak weekly) with your accounting team. Over the years I've encountered accounting individuals inside of companies who say they haven't seen or heard from the owner of the company in weeks unless the owner's credit card was denied or the owner needs some form of an emergency payment made to a vendor in order to continue to receive raw materials or services. Sometimes an unauthorized wire transfer of money is made because the sender thought someone in a leadership role did authorize the transfer, but no one communicated internally.

- Trust the members of your accounting team but do not have blind faith. Life is complicated. The pressures of life put a strain on us all. Some people resort to unethical or illegal behaviors up to and including embezzlement to try to work their way out of a personal hardship. You don't need to be paranoid or suspicious. Just be aware. Has a new bank account or corporate credit card been opened without your knowledge or consent? Is there someone in your accounting department who refuses to take a vacation or does not allow other authorized individuals to sign checks or make bank deposits? If you are the company owner do you know the passwords to your company's accounting software? Can you personally run your month end financial reports?

- Set a goal to have your accounting team get the month end financial reports to you within approximately 7 days of the close of the month. That target close date can be influenced by the size of your business, volume and type of transactions, and number of physical locations. You need that information in a timely manner so you can use it to make strategic decisions based upon the "story" that the numbers are telling. Receiving the month end close data in weeks instead of days renders the data practically useless. If billion-dollar corporations can close a month in approximately seven days so can your operation.

- Teach your entire team how their actions impact profitability. Not everyone directly drives revenue within an organization, but every one can help to control costs. Be aware of wasted time, wasted materials, idle, outdated, or obsolete inventory, and duplication of efforts (redundancy).

• Use accounting software and systems that are appropriate for your needs. At times proprietary software off the shelf at your local office supply store will do just fine. There may also be industry specific software available to you, perhaps with a related industry member discount. The easier the systems are to navigate the more likely people are to use them.

Chapter 10

"My Learning Days Are Over"

Throughout my career I've been fortunate enough to have worked in several industries including grocery, retail, hospitality, broadcasting, media sales, real estate sales, higher education, public speaking, and business consulting. Hence, I've attended hundreds of trade shows over the years as both a guest, an exhibitor, or a speaker.

My most vivid memories of trade shows come from the times when I was representing higher education (formal degree or adult learning programs). I was amazed (and honestly appalled) by the number of people who would wave their hands at me while never breaking stride while walking by my booth and proclaiming, "My learning days are over". Mind boggling.

Technically the most intelligent man I ever met was an astrophysicist. He once told me to envision measuring all the knowledge in the world by placing it in a box. Everything that every woman and man has known up to what everyone alive knows today…measured from the time when people first crawled out of caves. Pretty big box, right? Then he said "Here's the catch. Ever since knowledge has been measured the size of the box doubles every year and will continue to double annually into perpetuity. So how much do you think you know?"

Often when teaching or speaking I like to challenge the audience members. My challenge is this. "Tonight if your head is hitting the pillow and you're about to nod off (many of us are still clutching the TV remote) and you realize you haven't consciously learned something new today...get out of bed and teach yourself something!"

Our brains are like computer systems. My IT friends tell me that most computer users only tap into approximately twenty percent of the potential of their systems. Eighty percent of the system goes unused. As humans we're not tapping into the horsepower of the computers attached to our necks. As previously noted, the good news is that the human brain is wired to recognize patterns. That's why we do so many things automatically and without much thought. The bad news is that we do many things automatically and without much thought or learning.

We need to challenge ourselves to use more of the "bandwidth" of our brains.

Take Action Tips:

• Break your patterns. Force yourself to try a new exercise routine or take a different driving route to work. Introduce yourself to the new hires at your company. Learn about them.
• Seek new knowledge daily. Research indicates that the most productive and successful people in the world dedicate a minimum of five hours per week bettering themselves (learning). The majority of those learners do so very early in the day wrapped in the tranquility of peace and quiet with limited or no distractions.
• Make learning an expectation of your workplace. I often interview candidates for positions within my client companies. I like to ask

Millennials how they know when they've had a bad day at work. To date one hundred percent of them have answered "When I walk out the door and I realize I didn't learn anything new today." Millennials are hungry learners. They want to learn from you. The excuse of "It's not my job" to teach (sound familiar?) won't fly for long. They'll be out the door and headed to their next employment opportunity.

• Pass knowledge along. I absolutely believe that it is incumbent upon the leaders of today to help raise the next generation of leaders and thinkers. That means mentoring, tutoring, teaching, guiding and storytelling.

• Learn from the best. You can pay for lessons from a bad coach or pay more for lessons from a great coach. You get what you pay for.

• Seek out the individuals you deem to be successful (by your own standards and not necessarily society's standards) and pick their brains. Ask questions such as:

–"If you could reset your career, what would you do differently?"

– "Is there a course you wish you would have taken in high school or college that you didn't take?"

–"Where do you get information and data from?" "What sources do you trust?"

• Embrace YouTube (especially if you are a visual learner) and other learning platforms. Remember not everything on the internet is legitimate.

• Make learning fun! Network with peers within your industry and build mutually beneficial relationships with them. Expand your circle of influence outside of your industry. Join and be active in your area Chamber of Commerce. Meet politicians, clergy people, and teachers. Remember the phone book? Do you have a personal contact from nearly every category in the business section?

Chapter 11

"No One Does It Like I Do"

Confidence. I admire people with confidence. I strive to carry and conduct myself with confidence. People like to be around individuals who are confident and self-assured. We like to socialize, do business with, and recommend confident people.

We have to earn the right to be confident in ourselves as well as the right to have others place their confidence in us. There are times however when our confidence can work against us. If we believe too often that "No one does it like I do" (whatever "it" may be) we might cross that "line in the sand" where confidence becomes arrogance.

I'm sure we can all picture the people in our lives that are arrogant. They might be related to us. We may have worked alongside them. We may observe them from a distance or "know" them through the media. Nonetheless their arrogance repulses us. We don't want to be around them. We don't want to learn from them, and we certainly don't want to take direction from them.

An exaggerated belief in one's abilities and knowledge or perhaps outright arrogance can be detrimental to your own development and the success of your organization in several ways:

• You think you know it all, so you stop seeking learning experiences (see the previous chapter).

• You stifle creativity in your organization because you are doling out your "wisdom" before seeking input from others. Instead of generating ideas or potential solutions to challenges your teammates are simply handing back what's already been handed to them (directives from you disguised as brainstorming).

• People stop volunteering for activities like trade shows or face to face sales calls because they end up believing that their efforts will always pale in comparison to yours. That's what they believe because that's what you tell them (or word gets back to them that that's how you feel).

• You end up doing more work than you should (especially busy work versus strategic/creative work) because your trust that others can perform as well as you or better doesn't exist. Hence people let you shoulder the burden that you've become addicted to.

• The next wave of managers, leaders or owners of your organization are not adequately developed because you are attempting to clone yourself versus building upon the unique talents of the people surrounding you. You might want to work yourself into the position of being the least intelligent person at the table. That strategy may make succession planning much easier and potentially ensure the viability of your company into the future.

Take Action Tips:

• Give away credit. Take blame.

• Be confidently humble. If you're that good at what you do other people will spread the word for you.

• Get out of your own way. Give up some control to others. Your people know what to do (assuming you've hired the right ones). Let them run the business. If you are a "C" level individual or owner focus on strategically growing the business.

• Let someone else run meetings.

• Allow and encourage meetings to take place even when you are not physically available.

• Never stop building your network of talented resource people.

• Always make yourself available as a confident, trusted, and reliable resource to others (if you truly are).

• Know your limitations. Faking your way through challenges and circumstances often results in wasted time, effort, energy, and money while distracting you from the things you really could have accomplished with the knowledge, skills and experience you really do have.

• Surround yourself with people who are ready, willing, and able to tell you the truth when it comes to your strengths and weaknesses. These people should be a part of your Personal Advisory Board.

• Stop working and go home. Enjoy the people in your life, your hobbies and interests, and the fruits of your endeavors.

Chapter 12

"That Culture Stuff Is Crap"

In my opinion culture is one of those business topics that has no middle ground. You either believe whole heartedly in the power (positive or negative) of culture or you don't. When I consult, speak, or teach and the discussion moves to culture, people land on one side of the fence or the other.

All companies have a culture. It may be exceptional, great, good, mediocre, poor, or horrible. The combination of the quality of the people and their commitment to building and maintaining an exceptional culture is mission critical.

Culture has been defined in many ways over the years. Sometimes the word culture reminds us of our "roots" as people. Where we came from, the traditions we honor and the beliefs that we hold dear. Corporate culture in my opinion is what I call "workplace DNA". It's not what products we manufacture or services we provide. It's not our mission statement. It's not our vision statement. It's WHO WE ARE. How we treat each other, how we treat our customers, and how we expect to be treated. It's the internal expectations and standards that are set. It's about people.

Although I make my living spending significant amounts of time helping people and organizations create and execute strategies, I passionately believe that CULTURE TRUMPS STRATEGY EVERY DAY. A great business plan may fail inside of an organization that has a poorly defined or non-defined culture. A weak or average business plan in my opinion has a much better chance of being executed inside of an organization that has a strong culture.

Again, it's about the people. Within exceptional corporate cultures people step up, they take ownership, and they work outside of their job descriptions. They take results personally (with a healthy perspective), they embrace responsibility and accountability, and they drive change. Within such cultures people genuinely care about the work that's being done but they care even more about the people doing the work. They don't necessarily have to socialize together to feel like family. There's an inherent sense of pride that exists 24/7/365.

Many people can define their organization's mission and vision statements with some level of accuracy. Many people struggle when they are asked to describe (in their own words) the culture at that place they call work.

I'm old school enough to still read the Help Wanted section of the newspaper. Actually, it's no longer a section it's more like a few columns. Sometimes I challenge my clients, students, or seminar attendees to read every single Help Wanted ad in a local publication (or online for that matter) and circle every ad that describes a company's culture. I hope you're not investing in ink as not much will be used during that exercise.

Most ads still describe what the position entails, the work hours, physical location(s) of the enterprise, and the level of education required/desired. Most 7-year-olds can Google that information. Spend your money and advertising space describing your corporate culture. If the culture resonates with people, they'll dig deeper into the details of the position.

Take Action Tips:

• Spend the time (as much as needed) to define your corporate culture. Invite everyone within your organization to participate in this activity. Nothing screams non-inclusive louder than not asking someone at work for their opinion.
• Avoid the trap of being too flowery with the description of your culture. Think elevator pitch. Something people believe in and can remember, recite in their own words, and act upon daily. A few words that trigger thoughts, emotions, and action would be fine.
• Make sure what you describe and proclaim are true. Don't copy a culture statement that you like from another company. (Yes, it happens). This reminds me that over the years when I ask business people what the competitive advantage(s) of their companies are they quickly rattle off things like customer service, price, response time, and customer centricity. The same things most if not all their competitors say. At the end of the day many companies don't focus on their number one competitive advantage…their PEOPLE.
• Managers are in place to make sure that things get done the right way. Leaders are in place to make sure the right things get done. A mission critical task of the leader is to proclaim, profess, and protect the corporate culture each and every day.

- Again, Millennials now make up the largest percentage of the workforce (at least in the United States). They are attracted to culture and competent leadership more than salaries, benefits, and perks. (Although solid benefits are not frowned upon)! If you want to attract and retain Millennials it's imperative that you have a well-defined and healthy culture that doesn't just exist in theory on paper.

- The world changes. Economies change. People change. Technologies change. Take the pulse of your culture regularly. Make sure you're not living in the past trying to enforce cultural mindsets, behaviors, and practices that are outdated.

- Never stop looking for ways to improve the culture. The dividends on that mindset and the actions taken to build a "super culture" may produce the greatest returns your organization could ever generate.

- Work to build a "super workforce". Focus on combining the strengths of multiple generations to create and sustain a cohesive team.

- Have a well-organized onboarding process in place. Make people feel truly welcome on day one and not like afterthoughts added to the roster who need to be babysat.

- Allow peoples' personalities to shine through.

- Strive to make your company a "destination" company. A place where people want to work, are proud to work, and will recruit others to work at. Your culture must include being part of a greater good beyond what the purpose of the company actually is.

- Celebrate the victories, even the smallest ones. Not just work-related victories but people related ones as well.

Chapter 13

"I Plan On Working Forever"

Really? If that's what you say to yourself in your own head and that's what you tell other people I hope you feel this way because you LOVE your work, it's your passion, and you are making contributions of your time, energy, talents (and maybe money) to society for the betterment of the world. I hope you're not thinking and saying this because you're a slave to your job, it's the only thing you know how to do, you are not in a financial position to work less or not at all, and you have no passions to pursue or aspirations to chase beyond your work.

In the American culture we hope to earn enough money, save enough money, and stay healthy long enough to migrate to retirement. That's been the game plan for generations. For some people that plan works fine. Our world is ever changing. Some of my financial planner friends tell me that "People no longer retire. They get themselves to a place in life where they can afford to do what they always wanted to do."

The Millennial population is reframing the way we view and "do" work. Millennials don't live to work. They work so they can afford to experience the things that give them satisfaction now rather than in retirement. This group self-reports that they would prefer to own fewer material things in exchange for creating or having more life experiences. It makes sense. Millennials watched some of their parents and grandparents work like dogs to get to retirement. In retirement some of their relatives and friends fell ill, died, or saw their retirement savings decimated by unprecedented economic events. Millennials have taken on a "why wait?" attitude. To their credit they are using their knowledge, energy, and technology to get more work done faster. They are quite comfortable working from remote locations as well.

It's my belief that we have a perfect storm at hand in the workplace. A positive perfect storm. Seasoned "old school" workers and executives who planned on working forever are working alongside Millennials who comprise the largest sector of the workforce in the U.S. Why not start "passing the baton" earlier? In chapter 10 I noted that Millennials are hungry learners. I understand that not everyone can financially afford to work less or not work at all. Let's not jump that far ahead yet.

What I'm referring to is succession planning. I find it ironic that the word success is part of the word succession, yet most companies report that they don't have a succession plan or if they do have a plan it is poorly executed. Succession is one of those areas in business that some people think will magically work itself out.

Succession planning should be a fixture within your personal road map and corporate strategy. It should be crafted, reviewed, revised, and executed on a continuous basis.

Take Action Tips:

- Make sure that your organizational chart is accurate and current. It should be used in the succession planning process.
- Performance reviews (I trust you conduct them on a regular basis) provide the perfect opportunity to discuss career paths, aspirations, and succession planning with employees. If someone expresses an interest in taking on more responsibility or moving ahead in the organization make certain that you can detail the knowledge, experience, and education that they will need in order to potentially make that move. You should also highlight the personal sacrifices they may have to make that could also impact their families (more work, more travel, more stress?)
- Never assume that someone is interested in taking on different or additional responsibilities. As basic as this sounds, I've witnessed numerous occasions where it was assumed that an individual wanted to a part of advancement or succession and was never asked if they were interested. The process started, time and money were invested, and the process came to a screeching halt when the individual proclaimed "I never really wanted this!" Do everyone a favor and ask up front. Assuming is especially dangerous when it comes to family businesses. The kids and grandkids saw how hard their parents, grandparents, and other family members worked in the business. There's a good chance that they'll run fast in the opposite direction and never look back on the day they are asked if they are interested in taking over.
- Think short term, mid-term, and long-term when it comes to succession planning and your exit strategy. The particular stage where your business is at most likely will have unique needs and

initiatives that will require attention and direction from individuals with specialized talents. (Refer to the life cycle of businesses in chapter 7).

• If your plan is to one day sell your business remember these points:
  – Develop your management team now. The greatest asset a potential buyer should be interested in is your people (your greatest resource). Cash flow could be number two.
  – Plan to leave on your terms. Humble, confident and with a track record of success versus being shown the door or ousted by the Board of Directors after a vote of no confidence.
  – Align, strategize, and work with the best attorneys and CPAs. Your goals should be maximizing the value of your business and minimizing your tax consequences.
  – Use those same attorneys and CPAs to investigate whether an ESOP (Employee Stock Ownership Plan) is a viable option for your exit strategy. There are pros and cons to be weighed carefully.
  – You may consider the blood, sweat, and tears you poured into your business to be goodwill that you plan on being compensated handsomely for at the time of sale. Goodwill is an intangible asset that does not appear on the balance sheet. A potential buyer will not put the same value on goodwill as you do if they give it any consideration at all as part of the transaction.

Epilogue

So, there you have it. The thirteen most popular excuses that sabotage business success that I've heard repeatedly throughout my life as an employee, my career as a consultant, and my existence as a human. I'm sure there are plenty of other excuses that could fuel another book along with excuses yet to be created!

So now what? You've been given plenty of Take Action Tips in this book. Are you committed to doing things differently or are you comfortable creating and buying into excuses? A commitment to take action is like a New Year's Eve resolution. If you don't tell people about your resolution no one but you can hold you accountable. I urge you to tell people about your plans for action.

At the onset of my journey to write this book I told as many people as possible that I was writing a book. Yes, so they could regularly ask me how the book was coming along. Thanks to those of you who held me accountable!

Questions? Comments? Concerns? Feel free to visit www.speakingofstrategy.org and schedule a complimentary 20 minute chat.

I wish you wild success drenched in learning, laughter, and personal satisfaction. No Excuses!

- "Leadership Larry" Mietus

Acknowledgments

- Clients: Thanks for hiring me to be your trusted advisor. I appreciate your candor along with your confidence in me. WARNING: Some of these excuses may sound familiar.

- Mom and Dad: It took me a long time to realize that you did the best you could for us growing up with the resources that you had. I am who I am today because of you both. Miss you.

- Paulette ("Cheech"): My sister the warrior. You look adversity in the face and stare it down. I have always been and will always be proud of you.

- Scott Bieler: I'm honored to have you as a business colleague and friend. You are the true example of a servant leader. When in doubt I often say to myself "What would Scott do in this situation?"

- Center for Entrepreneurial Leadership at the State University of New York at Buffalo: Thanks for allowing me to work with a host of entrepreneurs throughout the years. I hope they learned a fraction from me of what I learned from them.

- Medaille College: Master of Arts in Organizational Leadership – Cohort 001. We took the leap of faith together. No regrets!

About the Author

Larry ("Leadership Larry") Mietus is the Founder of Speaking of Strategy. He is an independent business consultant, speaker, author, podcaster, and educator with a wealth of practical, hands on experience. His expertise encompasses leadership development, organizational design, employee engagement, and sales and marketing strategies. His clients run the gamut from "Mom and Pop" businesses to international enterprises. He is a frequent contributor on LinkedIn and numerous business blogs and has been featured on the Business Innovators Radio Network. Larry has also been quoted in HR Magazine, the most widely read and respected Human Resources publication in the world.

He self-designed his Bachelor's degree with a major in Sports Communication and minors in Advertising and Public Relations at the State University of New York at Buffalo (UB). He earned his Master's degree in Organizational Leadership at Medaille College.

Larry was twice named the "Mentor of the Year" by the Center for Entrepreneurial Leadership at UB. You can contact him at leadershiplarry@gmail.com | www.speakingofstrategy.org

Endorsements

"I just read *We Tried That Once.* I loved it! It was short and packed with information. Much of the information I have heard before, but it reminds me of things that we already are or should be doing. I like the action tips. I plan to use them as a to do list and make sure we are checking off every box. I will herein think of this book as the Thirteen Commandments of Business. Thanks for creating this concise, practical, and useful work!"

>   -Glen Donnarumma, D.D.S.,
>   Partner, Northtowns Oral & Maxillofacial Surgery, PLLC

"We Tried That Once" is a valuable source of concise information to help you improve and grow your business. It is a great reference of material for you and your team, to go back and review and refresh the necessary steps to manage your organization and to accomplish maximum results. I highly recommend Larry's book as a must read for you and your entire management team!"

>   -Scott Bieler
>   President & CEO, West Herr Automotive Group

"A great read for anyone looking to improve their leadership skills. Easy and fun to read...with practical solutions to everyday situations."

>   -Randy Strauss
>   Founder and Managing Partner
>   Strauss Group Executive Search Consultants

"As a business owner and human resources consultant, I found myself glued to *"We Tried That Once"* *And Other Popular Excuses that Sabotage Business Success!* Larry Mietus is a funny and engaging storyteller whose book is filled with relatable business excuses which hamper us from taking our businesses to the next level. The Take Action Tips included are critical for positioning one's business for success. This is a must read!"

-Lisa Stefanie, SPHR, SHRM-SCP
President, TripleTrack HR Partners

"We Tried That Once" is a roadmap for leaders who want to drive change in their organizations. Written with wisdom gathered from years of working with clients of all types, Larry has created an easy to read book that has tips for immediate implementation. Those of us who work with business clients have heard these excuses multiple times, and appreciate Larry distilling his experience into actionable steps that can make every business better."

-Susan Steffan
Chair of the Business, Management & Leadership Department at
Medaille College and founder, Steffan Solutions, a business consulting firm.

CPSIA information can be obtained
at www.ICGtesting.com
Printed in the USA
BVHW022312200221
600590BV00001B/2